THE VIEW FROM COLD MOUNTAIN

Poems of Han-shan and Shih-te

Translated by Arthur Tobias,
James Sanford and J.P. Seaton

Illustrations by Gyoskusei Jikihara

Edited by Dennis Maloney

White Pine Press

frontpiece illustration is from Goko Fugetsushu by Gyoskusei Jikihara
published by Sogensha; Osaka, Japan © 1970

Some of these translations have previously appeared in the *Greenfield Review,*
Ironwood and *White Pine Journal.*

Pinecone 13

Third Printing

ISBN 0-934834-26-1

Published by
White Pine Press
73 Putnam Street
Buffalo, New York 14213

Foreword

The Taoist/Zen hermits Han-shan and Shih-te stand among the poets of the spiritual such as Kabir, Rumi, Mirabai and Ryokan. They are poets whose poems move beyond mere religious sermonizing to encompass deep and powerful spiritual states while remaining personal in vision and statement.

Many years ago during my college days, when I was just beginning to write poems, I first came across the Cold Mountain Poems in a battered, used copy of Thomas Parkinson's **A Casebook on the Beat.** It contained Gary Snyder's translations of some 24 of the Han-shan poems which struck me with their direct and luminous qualities. The poems of Han-shan have continued to inform and delight over these many years.

The present volume brings together new translations of some of the Han-shan poems as well as poems by Han-shan and Shih-te that have never appeared in translation. As the introductions indicate there are and will remain questions as to the dates and true identities of Han-shan and Shih-te. Whether Han-shan and Shih-te were two men, several or the incarnates of the Bodhissattvas Manjusri and Samantabhadra matters little. What remains and what is of import are the poems, poems which point the way to our true nature, the boundless sphere.

It has been a pleasure, in the truest sense, to edit this collection and I wish to thank the translators for bringing these dharma songs into contemporary language. In addition, I also wish to thank the following members of the Sangha community for their help and assistance:

Gyoskusei Jikihara, Sensei - the master Zen sumi-e painter from Osaka, Japan who generously provided the paintings for the cover and frontpiece illustrations. He has traveled the world teaching sumi-e painting and in 1982, at age 79, journeyed to the United States to teach at the Zen centers of Los Angeles and Mt. Tremper.

Michael Hofman - painter and Jikihara, Sensei's translator and intermediary for his help and quick assistance in obtaining Jikihara's permission for the use of his paintings.

Diane Seijun Kay - a photographer and staff member of the Zen Arts Center in Mt. Tremper for photographing the cover painting by Jikihara, Sensei.

Andrew Taido Cooper and the staff of Ten Directions, the newsletter of the Zen Center of Los Angeles, where I first learned of Jikihara, Sensei's work. And who later provided a copy of the frontpiece illustration which was reprinted in Ten Directions from Jikihara's book **Goko Fugetsushu**.

Dennis Maloney
Matsu-an
August, 1982

Poems of Han-shan

Translated by Arthur Tobias

Han-shan

Not much is known for sure about Han-shan. Who and when remain mysteries; where is a much easier question to answer. Han-shan, literally "cold mountain", is part of the T'ien T'ai Mountains, a coastal range in northeastern Chekiang Province south of Hangchow and Hangchow Bay. What is known about Han-shan is that, judging from the internal linguistic evidence, there are two groups of poems in the collection. The earlier and larger portion contains about two thirds of its 300-odd poems. It also appears that there are differences in style and content between the two groups, with the latter portion tending toward religious sermons that aren't very good poems. The estimates on dating the collection vary from the mid sixth century to the mid ninth century. A late ninth century Ch'an (Zen) Master is known to have written a preface to a collection of 200 poems which supports the conclusions drawn from the linguistic evidence.

Han-shan, like many other mountain dwellers in Chinese history, took his name from the place where he lived. The only biographical information available comes from the poems themselves. One poem says that he left his home and family at the age of thirty, another says that he lived on Cold Mountain for thirty years. Gary Snyder, following the Japanese Zen monk commentators, treats him as a "Man Who Has Made It." Burton Watson, rejecting this view because of the way it forces interpretations of the poems, treats him as a "man on the Way." My own feeling is that the poems in the collection seem to record both the journey and the fruit. Each poem tells its own tale, and it's up to each reader to feel the quality of the energy within for him/herself. The selection of poems translated here seems to me to be representative of the collection as a whole. Happy climbing!

NOTES

The basic unit in Chinese poetry is the couplet, and in my translations I have maintained the original structure of the poems; each line contains the same information as its Chinese counterpart.

1.   Bells and cauldrons, large, heavy and expensive objects, were the possessions of the wealthy, and are representative of the pomp and circumstance of that kind of life. Line 4 was lifted intact from a poem by Hsieh Ling-yun (384-433), the father of Chinese landscape (literally, mountains and waters) poetry, noted for his Buddhism as well.

2.   Lu-ling literally means "law-command". In combination, the two graphs or characters are the name of a demon or spirit-being who was famous for his ability to run rapidly. As translated here, the last line is a Taoist incantory phrase which is probably the equilvalent of "faster than you can say 'Jack Robinson'." It is also possible to read this line as "as quickly as the law commands", a common last line for Buddhist charms and prayers, which is equally probable. Both readings fit the sense of the poem pretty well. The only reason for my choice is an affection for demons and spirit beings.

4.   Here, as elsewhere in Chinese poetry, the autumn moon is full. The full moon is a Buddhist symbol of enlightenment.

7.   The withered tree is an image with rich associations and a long history in Chinese literature. Here it is the symbol of something useless to human beings which is thus left alone to live out its life naturally without interference. This usage has its roots in the *Chuang Tzu*, and the image probably represents Han-shan himself. The last line refers to Chapter 1 of the *Chuang Tzu*, Free and Easy Wandering, in which there is a ming-ling tree for which 500 years make one spring, 500 years make one summer, etc., and a Rose of Sharon for which 8000 years make each season. The thrust of the question "how many years make one spring" points to the quality of the life that Han-shan experienced, the presence of the eternal in the present moment.

8.   The second line is a quote from Chapter 32 of the *Chuang Tzu*. The two brothers who starved to death, Po Yi and Shu Ch'i, did so because they objected to the use of force by the Chou dynasty to overthrow the Shang dynasty about 1100 B.C. Instead of serving the new dynasty, they fled to Shou-yang Mountain where they ate grasses and ferns, preferring a moral death to an immoral life. They are quite famous in Chinese literary history, and are the archetypes of the scholar-official who chooses an honorable death over a dishonorable life.

11.   The Yellow Springs is the underworld, the place where the dead go.

13. The purple mushroom, which is actually a fungus, supposedly gives immortality to those who eat it.

17. The pearl is the pearl of wisdom, another Buddhist symbol of enlightenment.

18. Mindless, or no mind, is a technical Buddhist term which refers to a state of consciousness without purpose or will, or the real immaterial mind free from illusion.

19. Kingfisher feathers were widely used for decoration because of their irridescent bluegreen color.

20. Buddhist monks were not supposed to look at themselves in mirrors.

22. The cave is the cave of the mind. The Dharmakaya is the impersonal body of Buddha, the Cosmic Buddha, or the body of the Law, the highest of the three bodies of Buddha in Mahayana Buddhist doctrine.

28. The blue-eyed foreigner is Bodhidharma, the First Patriarch of Chinese Ch'an (Zen) Buddhism.

1

Divination showed my place among these bunched cliffs
where faint trails cut off the traces of men and women
what's beyond the yard
white clouds embracing hidden rocks
living here still after how many years
over and over I've seen spring and winter change
get the word to families with bells and cauldrons
empty fame has no value

2

Everyone who reads my poems
must protect the purity of their heart's heart
cut down your craving   continue your days modestly
coax the crooked and the bent   then you'll be upright
drive out and chase away your evil karma
return home and follow your true nature
on that day you'll get the Buddhabody
as swiftly as Lu-ling runs

3

Looking for a place to settle out
Cold Mountain will do it
fine wind among thick pines
the closer you listen the better the sound
under them a man   his hair turning white
mumbling mumbling Taoist texts
he's been here ten years unable to return
completely forgotten the way by which he came

4

My heart is like the autumn moon
perfectly bright in the deep green pool
nothing can compare with it
you tell me   how it can be explained

5

Wanting to go to the eastern cliff
setting out now after how many years
yesterday I used the vines to pull myself up
but halfway there wind and mist made the going tough
the narrow path grabbed at my clothes
the moss so slippery I couldn't proceed
so I stopped right here beneath this cinnamon tree
used a cloud as a pillow and went to sleep

6

Sitting alone in peace before these cliffs
the full moon is heaven's beacon
the ten thousand things are all reflections
the moon originally has no light
wide open   the spirit of itself is pure
hold fast to the void   realize its subtle mystery
look at the moon like this
this moon that is the heart's pivot

7

I like my home being well hidden
a dwelling place cut off from the world's noise and dust
trampling the grass has made three paths
looking up at the clouds makes neighbors in the four directions
there are birds to help with the sound of the singing
but there isn't anyone to ask about the words of the Dharma
today among these withered trees
how many years make one spring

8

On his deathbed Chuang Tzu said
"Heaven and earth will be my inner and outer coffins"
when I return to where I've come from
some spirit money and a funeral pennant are all I'll need
when death takes me I'll feed the green flies
don't trouble the white crane to mourn
like the two brothers who starved on Shou-yang Mountain
if your life has been pure then death is also joyous

9

People ask the way to Cold Mountain
Cold Mountain   the road doesn't go through
by summer the ice still hasn't melted
sunrise is a blur beyond the fog
imitating me   how can you get here
my heart and yours aren't the same
if your heart was like mine
you'd return to the very center

10

I live beneath a green cliff
the weeds I don't mow flourish in the yard
new vines hang down all twisted together
old rocks rise up straight in precipitous slopes
monkeys pick the mountain fruit
egrets catch the pond fish
with one or two of the immortals' books
beneath the trees I mumble   reading aloud

11

The four seasons don't ever stop to rest
the years come and the years go
the ten thousand things succeed themselves endlessly
but the universe itself does not die or decay
the east is bright and the west is dark
flowers fall and flowers bloom again
only the travellers to the Yellow Springs
go shrouded in mystery and don't return

12

When the year passes   it's exchanged for a year of worries
but when spring arrives   the colors of things are fresh and new
mountain flowers laugh in green water
cliff trees dance in bluegreen mist
the bees and butterflies express their joy
the birds and fish are even more lovable
my desire for a friend to wander with still unsatisfied
I struggled all night but could not sleep

13

Your essays are pretty good
your body is big and strong
but birth provides you with a limited body
and death makes you a nameless ghost
it's been like this since antiquity
what good will come of your present striving
if you could come here among the white clouds
I'd teach you the purple mushroom song

14

There's a master who feeds on rosy clouds
he lives concealed from common wanderers
no matter what the season it's really restful
the summer is very much like the fall
hidden streams are always gurgling
the wind murmurs in tall pines
sit here for half a day
and you'll completely forget a hundred years' woes

15

If you're always silent and say nothing
what stories will the younger generation have to tell
if you hide yourself away in the thickest woods
how will your wisdom's light shine through
a bag of bones is not a sturdy vessel
the wind and frost do their work soon enough
plow a stone field with a clay ox
and the harvest day will never come

16

In the green creek spring water is clear
at Cold Mountain the moon's corona is white
silence your understanding and the spirit of itself is enlightened
view all things as the Void and this world is even more still

17

My resting place is in the deep woods now
but I was born a farmer
growing up simple and honest
speaking plainly without flattery
what nourished me wasn't studying for jade badges of office
but believing that a man of virtue would then get the pearl
how can we be like those floating beauties
wild ducks drifting on the waves as far as the eye can see

18

Clouds and mountains all tangled together up to the blue sky
a rough road and deep woods without any travellers
far away the lone moon a bright glistening white
nearby a flock of birds sobbing like children
one old man sitting alone   perched in these green mountains
a small shack   the retired life   letting my hair grow white
pleased with the years gone by   happy with today
mindless this life is like water flowing east

19

Yesterday   how long ago it seems
it was so lovely in the garden
above a path through peach and plum
below an island of orchid and iris
again the woman in the thin summer robe
her kingfisher feathers rustling in the pavillion
we met and I wanted to see her again
but my heart was pounding so that I could not speak

20

When people accept their bodies as the Source
then the Source uses their hearts to manifest its power
that the Source is alive in the heart is not false
but false hearts destroy the Source's commands
still unable to escape this disaster
why say you're reluctant to look in the mirror
don't chant the Diamond Sutra
and stop talking about the Bodhisattva disease

21

Back in the days when I had money
I was always lending it to you
now that you have acquired wealth
when you see me you don't try to share it
you must remember your own dreams and desires
which were just like the hopes that I have now
there is an affair that does not change —
I urge you to ponder it well my friend

22

In my house there is a cave
in the cave there's nothing at all
pure emptiness   really wonderful
glorious and splendid   bright as the sun
vegetarian fare nourishes this old body
cotton and hides cover this illusory form
let a thousand saints appear before me
I have the Dharmakaya for my very own

23

Despite the obstacles I pursued the great monk
the misty mountains a million layers high
he pointed to the road back home
one round moon   lantern of the sky

24

Ahead   the green creek sparkles as it flows
toward the cliff   a huge rock with a good edge for sitting
my heart is like a lone cloud   with nothing to depend on
so far away from the world's affairs
                    what need is there to search for anything

25

After all your talk of food   you're still hungry
after all your talk of clothes   you're still cold
eating rice is what fills your belly
wearing clothes is what keeps you warm
without really thinking it through
you grumble that the way to find Buddha is difficult
look inside your heart   there's Buddha
don't look for him outside your self

26

When this generation sees Han-shan
they all say I'm a crazy man
unworthy of a second look
this body wrapped only in cotton and hides
thay don't understand what I say
I don't speak their kind of jabber
I want to tell all of you passing by
you can come up and face Cold Mountain

27

Me   I'm happy with the everyday way
like the mist and vines in these rockstrewn ravines
this wilderness is so free and vast
my old friends   the white clouds   drift idly off
there is a road   but it doesn't reach the world
mindless   who can be disturbed by thoughts
at night I sit alone on a stone bed
while the round moon climbs the face of Cold Mountain

28

In my former days of bitter poverty
every night I counted other people's wealth
today I thought and thought then thought it through
everyone really must make their own
I dug and found a hidden treasure
a crystal pearl completely pure
even if that blue-eyed foreigner of great ability
wanted to buy it secretly and take it away
I would immediately tell him that
this pearl has no price

29

Amidst a thousand clouds and ten thousand streams
there lives one ex-scholar   me
by day wandering these green mountains
at night coming home to sleep beneath a cliff
suddenly spring and fall have already passed by
and no dust has piled up to disturb this stillness
such happiness   what do I depend on
here it's as tranquil as autumn river water

30

High   high   at the peak's tip
you can see forever in every direction
sitting alone   no one knows I'm here
the lone moon shines from a cold spring
but in the spring there's no moon
the moon itself is in the clear sky
yes   I sing this crooked little song
but in this song there's no Zen

31

I see people chanting a sutra
who depend on its words for their ability to speak
their mouths move but their hearts do not
their hearts and mouths oppose each other
yet the heart's true nature is without conflict
so don't get all tangled up in the words
learn to know your own bodily self
don't look for something else to take its place
then you'll become the boss of your mouth
knowing full well there's no inside or out

32

Cold Mountain is cold   ice locks up the rocks
hiding the mountain's bluegreen so it appears snow white
when the sun comes up   its light is immediately released
and this old traveller is nourished by its warmth

33

There's a clear wind among these bunched cliffs
the cold mist flows freely without a fan
the bright moon shines from its cage of white clouds
I'm sitting here all by myself   one old man

34

I see people in the world
who are each involved in emotional wrangling
one morning they're suddenly dead
and all they've attained is one plot of earth
four feet wide and twelve feet long
if you can come out of your grave and continue your wrangling
I'll put up your tombstone and write the inscription

Poems of Shih-te

Translated by

James Sanford and J.P. Seaton

Shih-te

Shih-te, whose name translates as "The Foundling", is traditionally seen as the ragged wildman companion of Han-shan. In the strictest Buddhist interpretation Han-shan and Shih-te are seen as the reincarnations of two divine figures, respectively Manjusri and Samantabhadra. Even more so than with Han-shan, and perhaps with very good reason, the facts of Shih-te's life are unclear, and likely to remain so. Modern scholarship seems to point to the possibility that several poets took, or had granted to their anonymous poems, the name Shih-te. These were monks or laymen who consciously modeled their works, and maybe their lives, on the life and work of Han-shan. This interpretation seems like a valid one, if only on the basis of the wide range of subject matter and the varying quality of the works assigned to Shih-te's creation. Shih-te, the one or many, was clearly Han-shan's spiritual companion and his poems share the rough hewn quality, the wit and the vigorous life which have made Han-shan immortal. Whether they are the work of one man, Han-shan's partner, of a Bodhissattva, Samantabhadra, or of a collection of monks and laymen on Han-shan's trail, they are good poems and real testaments to the Zen spirit.

NOTES

2. "The column that supports the universe", literally Mount Sumeru, the central peak in Buddhist cosmology.

4. prajna — the saving wisdom of Buddhism.

12. "Greed, anger, ignorance", literally the "three poisons" of Buddhism.

1

Since I came to this T'ien T'ai temple
how many Winters and Springs have passed
the mountains and the waters are unchanged
the man's grown older
how many other men will watch those mountains stand

2

I see a lot of silly folks
who claim their own small spine's
the column that supports the universe.
ants gnawing at a noble tree
never questioning their strength
they'll chew up a couple of Sutras
and pass themselves off as Masters
let them hurry and repent
from now on no more foolishness

3

see the moon's bright blaze of light
a shining lamp, above the world
full glistening and hanging in vast void
that brilliant jewel, its brightness, through the mist

some people say it waxes, wanes
their's may but mine remains
as steady as the Mani Pearl
this light knows neither day or night

4

prajna's wine, cold water, pure
drink deep, it sobers you
where I dwell, at T'ien T'ai side
those silly fools can't even see me
roam every valley deep
but never, where the world goes
no worry, no grief
no shame, and no glory

5

the Buddhas left their Sutras
because men are hard to change
it's not just a matter of saintly or stupid
each and every heart throws up its barricade
each piles up his own mountain of karma
how could they guess that what they clasp so close
is sorrow
unwilling to ponder, as day and night
they do embrace the falsehood of the flesh

6

sermons there are, must be a million
too many to read in a hurry
if you want a friend just come to T'ien T'ai mountain
sit deep among the crags
we'll talk about the Principles
and chat about dark Mysteries
if you don't come to my mountain
your view will be blocked
by the others

7

Han-shan's Han-shan
me, I'm Shih-te
how could the ignorant know us?
old Feng Kan, he thought he knew
but when he looked he couldn't see
and where he searched, he couldn't find us
you want to know how that could be?
in our way's the power of non-doing.

8

if you want to catch a rat
you don't need a fancy cat
if you want to learn the Principle
don't study fine bound books
the True Pearl's in a hemp sack
the Buddha nature rests in huts
many grasp the sack
but few open it.

9

I laugh at myself, old man, with no strength left
inclined to piney peaks, in love with lonely paths
oh well, I've wandered down the years to now
free in the flow; and floated home the same
　　　an unmoored boat.

10

not going, not coming
rooted, deep and still
not reaching out, not reaching in
just resting, at the center
a single jewel, the flawless crystal drop
in the blaze of its brilliance
the way beyond

11

free in T'ien T'ai's grotto
no seeker there will find me
Han Shan's my sole companion
chewing magic mushrooms, underneath tall pines
we chatter back and forth of old and new
sighing to think of all the others
each on his own way to hell
get your heads up, there's still time!

12

greed, anger, ignorance; drink deep
those poisoned wines and lie
drunk and in darkness, unknowing
make riches your dream
your dream's an iron cage
bitterness is cause of bitterness
give it up, or dwell within that dream
you better wake up soon
wake up, and go home.

13

a long way off, I see men in the dirt
enjoying whatever it is that they find in the dirt
when I look at them there in the dirt
my heart wells full of sadness
why sympathize with men like these?
I can remember the taste of that dirt.

14

when I was young I studied books and swordsmanship
and rode off with a shout for the Capital
there I heard the barbarians had all been driven off
there was no place left for heroes
so I came back to these crested peaks
lay down and listened to the clear stream flow
young men dream of glory:
monkeys riding on the ox's back.

15

cloudy mountains, fold on fold,
                    how many thousands of them?
shady valley road runs deep, all trace of man is gone
green torrents, pure clear flow, no place more full of beauty
and time, and time, birds sing
                    my own heart's harmony.

16

now your modern day monk's
fond of prating of love: hard core fool
starts out in search of getting free
and ends up somebody's lackey
morning to evening one mean hut to the next
praying and chanting for cash
making a bundle, and drinking it up
like any other shop-boy

17

if you want to be happy
there's no other way than the hermit's
flowers in the grove, endless brocade
every single season's colors new
just sit beside the chasm
turn your heads, as the moon rolls by
yet though I ought to be at joyous ease
I can't stop thinking of the others.

18

far, far, the mountain path is steep
thousands of feet up, the pass is dangerous and narrow
on the stone bridge the moss and lichen green
from time to time, a sliver of cloud flying
cascades hang like skeins of silk
image of the moon from the deep pool shining
once more to the top of Flowering Peak
there waiting, still
the coming of the solitary crane

19

Idle, I visited the high monks
green mountain, white clouds
next door crying children
on the other side a boisterous crowd

the Five-Peaks touch the Milky Way
the cobalt sky is clear as water
true, they pointed my way home
pool of lamplight beneath the moon.